SPANISH CIVIL WAR TANKS

The Proving Ground for Blitzkrieg

STEVEN J ZALOGA   ILLUSTRATED BY TONY BRYAN

First published in Great Britain in 2010 by Osprey Publishing,

Midland House, West Way, Botley, Oxford, OX2 0PH, UK

44–02 23rd St, Suite 219, Long Island City, NY 11101, USA

E-mail: info@ospreypublishing.com

A CIP catalog record for this book is available from the British Library

Print ISBN: 978 1 84603 512 8

PDF e-book ISBN: 978 1 84908 293 8

Page layout by: Melissa Orrom Swan, Oxford

Index by Mike Parkin

Originated by United Graphics Pte Ltd

Printed in China through World Print Ltd

10 11 12 13 14   10 9 8 7 6 5 4 3 2 1

FOR A CATALOGUE OF ALL BOOKS PUBLISHED BY OSPREY MILITARY AND AVIATION PLEASE CONTACT:

Osprey Direct, c/o Random House Distribution Center,
400 Hahn Road, Westminster, MD 21157
Email: uscustomerservice@ospreypublishing.com

Osprey Direct, The Book Service Ltd, Distribution Centre,
Colchester Road, Frating Green, Colchester, Essex, CO7 7DW
E-mail: customerservice@ospreypublishing.com

www.ospreypublishing.com

Osprey Publishing is supporting the Woodland Trust, the UK's leading woodland conservation charity, by funding the dedication of trees.

AUTHOR'S NOTE

The author would especially like to thank John Prigent, Oscar Bruña Royo, Mary Habeck, and Ken Estes for their help on this project.

CONTENTS

SPANISH CIVIL WAR TANKS
THE PROVING GROUND FOR BLITZKRIEG

INTRODUCTION

The Spanish Civil War was the first European conflict to see the extensive use of tanks since their debut in World War I. It came at a crucial time in European tank development, when production went from a few hundred tanks per year to many thousands. The Great Powers looked to the Spanish conflict to validate their own tank programs and to learn any important lessons about tank warfare. The Spanish Civil War has been regarded as the proving ground for blitzkrieg. Spain was seen as a laboratory for Germany, Italy, and the Soviet Union to test out their tanks and tactical doctrine on the eve of World War II.

The dominant tank in the Spanish Civil War was the Soviet T-26. This captured Republican T-26 Model 1937 was put on display in front of the Gran Kursaal in San Sebastián in 1938 after its capture near Tremp-Lérida. (NARA)

The Carro Veloce CV 3/35 was the most common version of the Italian tankette in service in Spain, though some of the earlier CV 3/33s were also used. The fasces marking on the superstructure side indicates a command vehicle. (NARA)

This book will argue that in fact the Spanish Civil War provided few clear tactical lessons. Tank employment in Spain was unique, and so no sober observer could draw any profound conclusions about the nature of future tank warfare. Tanks were used in relatively small numbers by poorly trained crews with little or no tactical understanding by senior commanders. Many armies did use the Spanish experience to validate their own preconceptions about tank warfare, but this was a misuse of the lessons. While the Spanish Civil War did not have a major impact on the development of tank doctrine, it had significant influence on tank design. The tanks used in the conflict were lightly armored and armed mostly with machine guns. The important exception was the Soviet T-26, which was armed with a powerful 45mm dual-purpose gun. This tank so dominated the Spanish battlefield that it ended once and for all the question about whether machine-gun-armed tanks were viable. They were not, and suddenly most European armies realized that their substantial investment in machine-gun-armed tanks in the early 1930s was seriously flawed.

Spain also saw the first widespread use of dedicated antitank guns, notably the German Rheinmetall 37mm and its Soviet copy, the 45mm antitank gun. When skillfully used, these weapons could prove to be an effective counter to rampaging tanks. While the Spanish conflict did not decisively demonstrate the relative balance between tank and antitank warfare, it strongly suggested that the cheap and lightly armored tanks of the 1930s were too vulnerable. The lessons of the war spurred the production of medium tanks, which would form the steel core of Europe's armies in World War II.

TANK TECHNOLOGY ON THE EVE OF WAR

In the wake of World War I, most European armies neglected further tank development. An ample supply of tanks was still on hand from the war, and the meager defense budgets of the 1920s did not encourage expensive new programs. Germany was forbidden tanks under the Versailles Treaty and the Soviet Union was still licking its wounds after a debilitating civil war. Tank development began to accelerate in the early 1930s. The World War I tanks had been mechanically arthritic even in their prime, and by the 1930s were mostly worn out.

A PzKpfw I Ausf A of the 1st Batallón de Carros de Combate in Vergara during operations in the Basque country against the Army of the North in 1938. (John Prigent Collection)

The T-26 was a license-built copy of the British Vickers 6-ton export tank, but fitted with a Soviet-designed turret armed with a 45mm gun derived from the German Rheinmetall 37mm antitank gun. The crew was three: a driver in the hull, and a gunner and loader/commander in the turret. This example is a captured T-26 in service with the 1st Batallón de Carros de Combate de la Legion in 1938. (NARA)

Britain had been at the forefront of tank development in World War I, and was the most influential tank manufacturing country in the early 1930s. This was due not only to its weapons firms such as Vickers, but also to its visionary military thinkers such as J. F. C. Fuller, who wrote extensively on the nature of future war and the equipment needs of modern armies. One of the most influential developments in Britain was the Carden-Loyd tankette. This was a small, two-man vehicle armed with a single machine gun. From a tactical standpoint, these inexpensive tankettes could be built in large numbers and swarm over the battlefield in force. This was in fact an elaboration of the concepts of the French general Jean-Baptiste Estienne, which had spawned the Renault FT tank in 1917. Regardless of its tactical merits, the tankette idea was popular in Europe because such vehicles were so cheap. They seemed like a prudent choice when defense budgets were so meager. The Soviet Union adopted the Carden-Loyd under license as the T-27, Italy made a copy as the CV 3/33, and Poland built its own example as the TK. These tankettes were the most widely produced armored vehicles of the early 1930s and the Italian CV 3/35 would see extensive service in Spain.

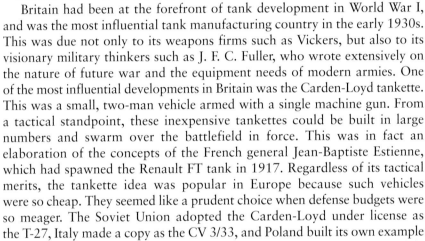

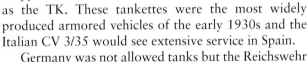

Germany was not allowed tanks but the Reichswehr experimented with armored chassis under the guise of artillery tractors. Krupp had been given a contract to develop a light tractor in 1931 that was the surreptitious basis for a future tank. After Hitler came to power in 1933, the Versailles Treaty restrictions were renounced and the Krupp light tractor emerged as Nazi Germany's first tank, the Panzerkampfwagen I (PzKpfw I). This tank was significantly larger than tankettes and had a traversable turret. Technically, it was a further evolution of the French Renault FT of 1917 but with more modern automotive design. German tank design in 1917–18 had focused on the construction of small numbers of very large tanks, epitomized by the A7V, but these designs were clumsy and too costly. After this mistake during World War I, German opinion swung in favor of Estienne's view that a "bee swarm" of inexpensive tanks was more valuable than a handful of massive tanks. The PzKpfw I satisfied this tactical

objective and was also essential in providing German industry with the technical lessons that would be needed for larger and more elaborate designs. The PzKpfw I was never designed to fight other tanks, since there had been hardly any instances of tanks fighting other tanks during World War I. The PzKpfw I was another of the interwar tank types to see extensive combat in Spain.

Another influential tank in the interwar years was the Vickers 6-ton tank. This was a commercial design intended for export, and the British Army never bought any significant number. It was sold to the Soviet Union, Poland, the United States, China, and several other countries. It inspired many World War II tank designs, including the US Army's M3 Stuart, the Italian M11/39 and M13/40, and the Polish 7TP. Its most important evolution was the Soviet T-26 light tank. As a commercial export product, several armament options were offered, including the Model A "trench clearer" fitted with two turrets, each with a light machine gun; the Model B "fire support" tank fitted with a single turret and short 47mm gun; and the Model C "tank destroyer," which was configured like the Model A but had long 37mm antitank guns in the hull. The Soviet Union bought license production rights for the Vickers in 1930. Since the Red Army planned to deploy the T-26 for infantry support the twin-turret layout was selected, so that the tank could then engage two targets simultaneously. Although tank-vs-tank fighting was not considered a major tactical concern, work began in 1932 on a T-26 tank destroyer fitted with a single large turret armed with a 45mm antitank gun. An important innovation in this design was the incorporation of a coaxial machine gun with the antitank gun, which permitted the crew to engage targets with

Many of the T-26s sold to Spain were the latest 1937 production type, which included a P-40-UM antiaircraft machine gun mount for a Degtaryev light machine-gun on the right side of the turret roof. The DT machine gun mounted in the turret rear was a feature added in 1935. This is a captured Nationalist tank with the 1st Batallón de Carros de Combate de la Legion. (NARA)

gunfire, machine-gun fire, or both. It is worth digressing a moment to explore the origins of the gun selected for the T-26 as it helps illuminate some broader tactical trends in European weapons at the time.

The Soviet 45mm tank gun was a spin-off from another program: the Red Army's effort to arm its infantry with a modern antitank gun. During the late 1920s and early 1930s there was considerable debate about the ideal weapon to equip the infantry to fight tanks. Many armies adopted an antitank rifle for small-unit defense and the Red Army did the same. A longer-range and more powerful weapon was sought for battalion and regimental defense. Some armies, such as Italy's, opted for a dual-purpose 47mm gun that could fire a worthwhile high-explosive round as well as an antitank projectile; other armies such as those of Britain and France preferred a dedicated antitank gun optimized for antitank projectiles. The Red Army purchased the rights to the German Rheinmetall 37mm in 1930, and it entered small-scale production in 1931 as the 1-K 37mm Model 1930 antitank gun. However, Red Army officers argued that it would be more useful as a "universal gun" if it could fire a better high-explosive projectile. The 37mm round was quite weak, with only a 20g high-explosive charge so it was scaled up to 45mm with double the high-explosive fill in the enlarged projectile. It entered production in 1932 as the 19-K 45mm Model 1932 antitank gun.

In 1933 the 19-K was modified as the 20-K, which was essentially the same weapon but adapted for use on armored vehicles. Tests of the weapon in an enlarged T-26 turret went smoothly, and senior Red Army commanders were enthusiastic about such a design as a "universal infantry tank" rather than as a tank destroyer, since the combination of a dual-purpose 45mm gun and a coaxial machine gun allowed the tank to engage a wide variety of enemy targets at much longer ranges than the existing twin-turreted T-26. As a result, production of the T-26 began to shift to the new single-turret version in the summer of 1933. This version is erroneously called the T-26B in many accounts. In fact, the Red Army was very parsimonious with official designations, and official documents distinguish three types: the T-26 *dvukhbashenniy* (twin-turret); the T-26 *lineyniy* (line); and the T-26 *radiyniy* (radio), with the later two types armed with the 45mm gun. This book will refer to them by the terms used in recent Russian accounts by their production year. The T-26 raised the stakes in the European arms race of the 1930s, as would become clear in Spain.

THE PRE-WAR DINOSAURS

1. Carro de Artilleríe Schneider CA1, Madrid, 1936

In 1926, the Spanish Army adopted gray as the standard color for its vehicles, which were sometimes nicknamed "Tiznado" as a result. The Schneiders had been put into reserve before the war due to their poor mechanical state, but saw some combat use in the initial fighting in 1936, including the attack on Cuartel de la Montaña. Protected trucks and some tanks, such as the Schneider here, were decorated with the names of the political militias that provided crews, in this case the Unión General de Trabajadores and Unión de Hermanos Proletarios.

2. Trubia A4, Regimiento de Infantería Milán número 32, Oviedo, 1937

The three pre-series Trubia A-4 tanks were attached to an infantry regiment in the Oviedo region, probably due to the proximity to the Trubia plant where they were manufactured. They belonged to the Republican Army of the North during the fighting in Asturias in 1937, where they were captured eventually by the Nationalists. Photos show them in a dark finish, which may have been dark gray or olive drab, as shown here based on recent Spanish depictions.

1

2

TANKS IN SPAIN

Spain had been in the backwater of European military developments for more than a century. It had a dozen Renault FT light tanks and six of the heavier Schneider CA1 tanks from France in the years after World War I. The Renault FTs were dispatched to Morocco in 1921 to support the Spanish Foreign Legion (Tercio de Extranjeros) in its fight against the Rif rebellion. A young officer of the 1st Batallón (1a Bandera) of the legion, Major Francisco Franco, remarked, "Armored cars and tanks are well suited for this war. We shall see if time proves me right." In fact, the first tank action on March 17, 1922, was discouraging. The tanks advanced in front of the infantry due to their higher speed, but a number proved useless in combat when their machine guns jammed. Two tanks broke down and were left behind, only to be blown up by the Rif with dynamite. This combat debut had several clear lessons. Tanks were not miracle weapons, even when used against poorly armed rebels. Tanks could not hold ground on their own without proper coordination with the infantry. Mechanical reliability issues as much as tactical issues remained the bane of early tank operations. The Renaults were reinforced by the six Schneiders in 1923. The tanks saw small-scale use over the next few years, and the FT tanks took part in the bold amphibious landings on Alhucemas Bay in September 1925, a major victory in the pacification campaign. While the use of tanks in the Rif war attracted little attention in the outside world, it had considerable influence on ambitious young officers of the Foreign Legion like Franco, who would play critical roles in the later civil war.

Following the Rif War, the tanks returned to Spain. The Moroccan campaign had excited enough interest to inspire tank manufacture in Spain. The Trubia tank was manufactured at the Fábrica Nacional de Trubia in 1925. It resembled an enlarged Renault FT but with three machine guns. After initial trials, the improved Carro Ligero Trubia A4 went into pre-series production with four examples built. Tanks were associated with the artillery,

The Spanish Army acquired six French Schneider CA1 tanks in the early 1920s, which were used in the Rif War in Spanish Morocco. The Republicans had four in Madrid, including this one, and the Nationalists had the other two in Zaragoza. (Author's collection)

and after an abortive coup by artillery officers in 1926, their programs fell out of favor. Spain purchased samples of other tanks in the 1920s, such as an Italian Fiat-3000A light tank in 1924, essentially an Italian copy of the Renault FT. During the Asturias Rebellion in 1934, the Trubia plant converted five Landesa tractors into improvised tanks, the Carro Armado Landesa, by constructing an armored superstructure on the chassis. It was fitted with a single machine gun in the casemate. When the civil war started in 1936, most surviving tanks belonged to the Regimiento Ligero de Carros de Combate (LCC) número 1 stationed near Madrid, and Regimiento LCC número 2, near Zaragoza.

The Regimiento LCC número 1 based near Madrid sided with the Republic and was used in some of the early actions of the war including Sierra de Guadarrama (July 1936), where one of their Renault FT tanks is seen derelict after the fighting. (Oscar Bruña Royo)

Although Spanish tank production was meager, there was a continual interest in the production and use of protegido camión (protected trucks). Unlike the more familiar armored car, these vehicles were for the most part built using non-armor steel or iron plate, which offered limited protection against small arms. Numerous types were built in small batches in the 1920s in Spain and Morocco, and they were used for convoy escort and other secondary military tasks. Production of protected trucks accelerated in the early 1930s due to the growing political unrest in Spain. With the abdication of the king and the creation of the Second Republic in the summer of 1931, political violence reached fever pitch. The October 1934 revolt in Asturias led to the construction of more than a dozen protected trucks. Various state police forces began ordering protected trucks for riot control, and a number of political militias also constructed their own examples. The new Republican government formed the Guardia de Asalto, a paramilitary riot-police force equipped mainly with small arms, but a motorized section with armored cars

The Bilbao armored car was the only mass-produced armored vehicle in Spain before the war. It was a simple design, intended more for internal security duties than battlefield use. These two examples are in Nationalist units in the 1938 fighting. (NARA)

was also planned. To equip these units, the Sociedad Española de Construcción Naval (SECN) developed the Camión Blindados Bilbao Modelo 1932 armored car on the basis of imported Dodge K32 trucks. This was a lightly armored vehicle with a 7mm Hotchkiss machine gun in a simple turret and at least 45 were completed. Some were built for the cavalry and served with the Grupo de Autoametralladoras-Cañón of the cavalry division in Aranjuez near Madrid.

ORIGINS OF THE SPANISH CIVIL WAR

While this book does not have the space to discuss the complex origins of the war in Spain, a basic summary is helpful to better appreciate the tank warfare that took place. Following the end of the Spanish monarchy in 1931, Spain attempted to establish a parliamentary democracy, with little success. Lacking a democratic tradition, Spanish politics were bitterly polarized by the political extremes of right and left. The government in 1936 was controlled by the Popular Front, a left-wing alliance including liberal, socialist, trade-unionist, and communist parties. The left's anti-clerical excesses aggravated the more traditional elements of society and led to plans for a military coup by the army, supported by various conservative, monarchist, and clerical parties.

The Spanish Army at the time was modest in size – about 100,000 troops, of which 30,000 belonged to the Army of Africa in Spanish Morocco. The metropolitan army was a poorly trained and poorly led conscript force, with most ambitious officers serving in the colonies. It was so ineffective that the government had been forced to create paramilitary security units to quell the political violence that wracked Spain through the 1930s. The army in Morocco included most of the professional units, with a core of experienced colonial troops, as well as the battle-hardened Legion. Not surprisingly,

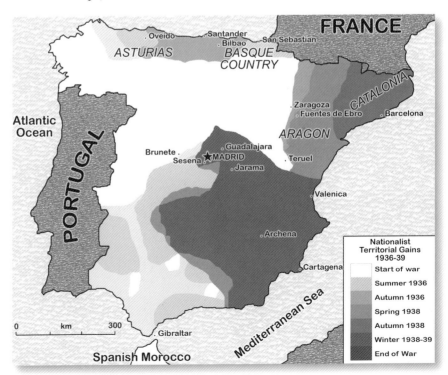

Map of the battle zone

the muscle of the rebel movement against the Popular Front government came from the Army of Africa. The nominal head of the coup forces was General José Sanjurjo, the "Lion of the Rif," who had commanded the bold Alhucemas amphibious landings in 1925. The coup was launched on July 18, 1936, starting in Spanish Morocco, after which the colonial units began their move to the Spanish mainland. The rank and file of the Spanish Navy proved less enthusiastic to the rebel cause than the Army of Africa, and when instructions were sent to dispatch the navy's warships to Morocco to lift the army to Spain, the lower ranks refused and sided with the Republic. In an act that would presage the later Great Power involvement in the conflict, on July 22 Hitler agreed to send Junker Ju-52 transports to Morocco to help lift Franco's forces into Spain. By the end of July the civil war was in full swing, with Nationalist rebels in control of much of western and northern Spain.

Although the rebels started the war with serious numerical disadvantages, they enjoyed the advantage of unity and a disciplined military force. Besides the 30,000 troops of the Army of Africa, about half of the metropolitan army rallied to their side, along with most of the officers. Of the 65,000 paramilitary troops, more than half sided with the Nationalists, including a majority of the Carabineros and Civil Guard. There was also greater political unity between the various political factions backing the Nationalist rebels, including conservative, royalist, and Catholic parties.

The Republican side controlled about two-thirds of Spanish territory, including most of the major cities and industry. The navy sided with the Republic as did the merchant marine, which controlled the vital export trade. The government also controlled the gold reserve, which was essential for purchasing arms from abroad. In spite of these advantages, the Republic was beset by enormous military problems. It eventually formed the Ejército Popular Republicano (EPR: People's Republican Army) based on the bedraggled remnants of the army and security forces that had remained loyal, combined with various political militias. These units were enthusiastic but poorly led and completely untrained. The Republican forces were an uneasy coalition of fractious leftist parties that were often at each other's throats; furthermore, the alliance also contained separatist regions such as the Basque country and Catalonia.

A pair of CV 3/33 tankettes of the Italian CTV's Raggruppamento Carristi moving forward in 1938. This is the earlier version of the tankette and not as widely seen in Spain as the CV 3/35. (NARA)

Neither Britain nor France wanted to be dragged into the conflict, and promoted a non-intervention policy. While this was honored by some of the major powers, Italy and Germany quickly aligned themselves with the Nationalists, while the Soviet Union aligned with the Republicans. These three nations would become the main source of advanced weapons and "volunteer" troops during the ensuing conflict. The Republican cause became a political rallying point of the trade-unionist and leftist parties around Europe, and led to the creation of the International Brigades, made up of foreign volunteers.

INITIAL BATTLES FOR MADRID

The small numbers of armored vehicles available in Spain in 1936 meant that neither side had a significant tank force at the beginning of hostilities. The Republicans inherited the greater share of armored vehicles, but this offered little advantage. The old Renault and Schneider tanks were not mechanically reliable, nor were the small numbers of Spanish-built tanks such as the Trubia. The Bilbao armored cars, while relatively numerous, were essentially road-bound and poorly armed. The Regimiento de Carros número 1 in Madrid stayed on the Republican side, while Regimiento número 2 in Zaragoza sided with the Nationalists.

Spanish Armored Forces, Summer 1936		
Type	Republican	Nationalist
Schneider CA1	4	2
Renault FT	9	6
Fiat-3000A	1	0
Trubia	1	3
Landesa	2	0
Bilbao	41	5

The outbreak of the war led to the construction of hundreds of protected trucks, especially by Republican militias in the industrial areas. In total, factories under Republican control built at least 400 protected trucks; one document lists no fewer than 159 constructed in Catalonia alone in 1936–37. These were a mixed blessing. Although they were sometimes used with daring and boldness, they were often poorly designed and prone to breakdown. The truck chassis were overburdened by the steel or iron plate that led to engine overheating and automotive collapse; the narrow tires combined with the excessive weight meant that the protected trucks had very high ground pressure, and so could not be used off the road except on exceptionally hard and flat terrain; they were top-heavy and prone to overturning. In later

A Spanish crew prepares a T-26 Model 1933. This is a fairly early production example from the original batches with the Vickers-pattern road wheels. (Patton Museum)

years, true armored cars manufactured with armor plate were built, and these are detailed later.

The first batch of new tanks to arrive in August 1936 came from Italy, consisting of a platoon of five CV 3/35 tankettes and crew. They were dispatched to the port of Vigo in Galicia, in northwestern Spain, and put under the control of the Nationalist Army of the North. Since the Italian government initially forbade Italian troops from participating in combat, the Italian tankers trained Spanish volunteers. These tankettes took part in the occupation of San Sebastián but saw no actual fighting. A second Italian contingent arrived on September 29, consisting of a company of ten tankettes with three flame-thrower tankettes. Captain Oreste Fortuna and his troops volunteered to join the Tercio in order to see combat and were sent to the Madrid front. They first saw combat on October 21, 1936, at Navalcarnero near Madrid, where their unexpected appearance rattled the Republican defenders and led to a rout. The company was subsequently honored as the Compañía artillería-legionaria "Navalcarnero."

While the Italian tankers were seeing their combat debut in the outskirts of Madrid, the first shipment of tanks had arrived from the Soviet Union at Cartagena on October 12, 1936. This included 50 T-26 light tanks, some BA-3 armored cars, and 51 "volunteer" tank specialists. The Soviet government did not plan to provide enough crews for the tanks sent to Spain, but rather to train Spanish personnel to operate them. Archena became the main training and technical center for the Republican tank force for most of the war and was originally headed by Kombrig (Brigadier) Semyon M. Krivoshein. In spite of the original plans to restrict the Soviet tankers to training duties, the situation of the Republican forces around Madrid was so desperate in late October that Moscow authorized Krivoshein to deploy some ad hoc combat formations. At least three small groups were dispatched to the Madrid front, one headed by Komrot (Captain) A. Novak, with six BA-3 armored cars and seven T-26 tanks, a Spanish tank platoon under Major P. Villakansas, and a reinforced company-sized formation under Kombat (Major) Paul Arman. The two first groups went into action on the night of October 27, 1936, with little impact.

The first significant action by the Republican tank force involved Arman's partially formed 1st Tank Battalion. Arman had selected the best Soviet crews,

A column of T-26 Model 1933 tanks from Krivoshein's Aranjuez Group during the defense of Madrid in 1936. (Patton Museum)

mixed with some of the new Spanish crews, for a total of 34 Soviet tankers and 11 Spanish crewmen. Arman is reported to have proclaimed, "The situation is not so hopeless. They have 15,000 soldiers, we have 15 tanks, so the strengths are equal!" On the morning of October 29, 1936, Arman's company supported an attack by two Republican infantry brigades against Italian and Spanish Nationalist units in the village of Seseña, on the southern approaches to Madrid. This attack displayed the problems and potential of the tactical employment of tanks in the Spanish conditions.

The Spanish infantry had no training to operate with tanks, and Arman had no patience to wait for them. Of his 15 tanks, three were disabled almost immediately by mines on the road to the town, a novel experience as antitank mines had been a relative rarity in World War I. Pressing ahead, Arman bluffed his way past a battery of Nationalist field guns in the western outskirts of Seseña and his forces then attacked the main Nationalist positions in the town itself. One of his tanks was destroyed in the street fighting when struck by a flaming bottle of gasoline. This was the first time Molotov cocktails had been used in combat in Spain and had been prompted by the debut of the other Soviet armored units a few days before. After shooting up the Nationalist forces in the village, Arman led his company out of town eastward in an attempt to strike at the rear of the Nationalist forces. After overrunning a field-gun battery, the T-26 tanks encountered three CV 3/35 tankettes of the Italian Compañía Navalcarnero. Two tankettes were armed only with machine guns and one with a flame-thrower, and their counterattack against Arman's force was doomed. The flame-tankette, commanded by P. Baresi, attempted to approach close enough to the Soviet tanks to use its flame-thrower, but was blasted with gunfire. Another tankette was pushed into a ditch and overturned by a much larger T-26 tank.

During the raid Arman's group lost three tanks to Molotov cocktails and artillery fire, with three more damaged; and it suffered casualties of four Soviet and four Spanish tankers killed, and six wounded. Arman claimed that his group had destroyed two infantry battalions and two cavalry squadrons, ten 75mm field guns, two tankettes, 20–30 trucks, 5–8 automobiles, and some tank transporters, and captured two field guns. Although Arman's raid was an important psychological boost for the harried Republican forces, the Republican attack was a failure due to the inability of the infantry to fight their way into the town, lacking the promised tank support. The poor coordination of tank and infantry at Seseña would prove typical of the Spanish experience. On the Nationalist side, the Italian tankettes continued to see combat action for the next several weeks, but were withdrawn from the front in late November after four were lost. After several more days' fighting on the outskirts of Madrid, the scattered Republican tank formations were united by Kombrig Krivoshein to form the Aranjuez Group, though in practice the unit's companies were dispersed to support various Republican brigades, including the fighting in Madrid itself in December 1936. The

B **T-26 MODEL 1933, ARANJUEZ GROUP, MADRID, NOVEMBER 1936**
Krivoshein's Republican battalion at the time of the Madrid fighting had extremely simple markings, usually a two-digit tactical number painted on the hull front, either side of the turret, and sometimes on the hull rear. This particular example was more colorfully marked than most, with slogans on the turret and hull side: "Viva el Ejercito del Centro" (Long live the Army of the Center) and "Viva Madrid." The communist hammer-sickle was sometimes applied to Republican tanks. The finish is the usual pre-war Soviet-camouflage dark green.

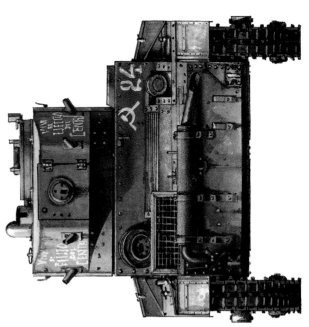

Italian tankers inspect a Republican T-26 knocked out during the fighting. The small Italian CV 3/35 was no match for the larger and much better-armed Soviet tank. (Patton Museum)

Spanish Renault FT tanks were consolidated in a company under D. Pogodin to support Krivoshein's tanks during the Madrid fighting.

The Republic rebuffed Franco's attack on Madrid and there was almost universal praise for the performance of Krivoshein's scattered tank units. The Soviet advisory team in Madrid sent this assessment to the Kremlin: "Arman's tanks group created real miracles. It is possible to say with complete assurance that if the fighter group and Arman's tanks would not have been present during the first period of the defense of Madrid, the defense of the city would have been an exceptionally catastrophic situation. It is impossible to adequately describe the heroism of the tankers; they prevented the retreat of the infantry; they were always in the vanguard; they fought single-handedly with enemy gun batteries, and they demolished the battle plans of the opponent. They always took best advantage of the tanks in infringement of all technical and authorized norms and never refused or questioned orders to carry out a task. Tanks fought all day long; returned to the support area at night to repair the vehicles and during the morning returned to the fight."

By mid-December 1936, Krivoshein's small armored force was largely spent, due not only to battlefield casualties, but also to the mechanical exhaustion of the tanks themselves. Soviet tanks of the 1930s were not very robust; the T-26 light tank required intermediate overhaul at district workshops after 150 engine hours, and factory overhaul after 600 hours. Tracks and track pins began to wear out after 800km of travel; side clutches became worn; and the powertrain was gradually knocked out of alignment from hard cross-country travel. In the desperate fighting during the defense of Madrid, Arman's company had accumulated over 800 operating hours by mid-December, far beyond the regulations, leaving many of its tanks inoperable. Krivoshein's other units were not in much better shape, as the inexperienced Spanish crews were unable to do field repairs, and their unfamiliarity with tank driving led to high rates of clutch and powertrain failures. There were no established maintenance facilities in the Madrid area, and spare parts were almost nonexistent. While Krivoshein's tank force had succeeded in its immediate mission of bolstering the Republican forces during the defense of Madrid, this was no way to operate a tank force for prolonged campaigns.

It became clear from the initial fighting that tank units could not be employed nonstop, day and night like infantry, but had to be carefully husbanded for only the most important missions. The experience with the new Spanish tank crews was discouraging, and the Red Army practice of assigning a junior crewman to driving duties usually left them in

the hands of inexperienced Spanish crewmen. This led to abnormally high breakdown rates, and forced Krivoshein's unit to reorganize crew tasks, with Russian tank commanders shifted to the driver's position in the hope of keeping the tanks operable. However, this adversely affected the combat capabilities of the tanks, since the more experienced Soviet tanker was unable to command the tank and direct the gunner from the isolation of the driver's station.

Cooperation between the tanks and the infantry was almost uniformly abysmal. There was no training by the tanks and infantry in cooperative tactics before missions, and the tank companies seldom worked with the same infantry unit for more than a few days, so no experience was accumulated. The Republicans could not afford to pull the tank companies out of the line for such training, and Krivoshein's units were reluctant to expend precious engine hours drilling with the Spanish infantry. Krivoshein and Arman were ordered back to Moscow to brief senior Red Army leaders in January 1937.

The violent fighting around Madrid in the autumn of 1936 convinced most of the interventionist governments to drop the fig leaf of "volunteer" troops.

The Italian tankette companies in Spain were supported by smaller numbers of the Lancia 1ZM armored cars in a Squadriglia Autoblindo. This was a modernized version of an armored car originally built during World War I. (NARA)

Von Thoma's Panzergruppe Drohne was a training establishment and the German tank crews saw very little tank combat. Here, German crews instruct a Spanish soldier on a PzKpfw I Ausf B. (John Prigent Collection)

On December 13, 1936, Mussolini agreed to send entire Italian units to fight in Spain, eventually forming the Corpo Truppe Volontarie (CTV: The Corps of Volunteer Troops). The Italian armored contingent expanded continually as a result. A second tankette company arrived in November 1936, a squadron of eight Lancia 1ZM armored cars in late December 1936, and two more tankette companies in January 1937. The expanded tankette force formed the Battaglione Carri d'Assalto per Oltre Mare Spagna (OMS: Spanish Overseas Tank Battalion). In February 1937 this battalion was incorporated into the larger Raggruppamento Reparti Specializzati (RRS: Specialist Unit Group), which also included motorized artillery, motorized infantry, and an armored-car company. The creation of the RRS was clear evidence of the subordinate role that tankettes played in the CTV, being lumped together with other technical supporting arms. There was little effort made to create a fast mobile force during the first year of the fighting. The battalion was split into two weak battalions later in 1937, each with only two companies. This was typical of the Spanish experience, with the CTV dispersing its limited tank support due to widespread demand on scattered fronts.

Germany was the third major power to intervene and deployed the smallest tank contingent, largely overshadowed by its aviation counterpart, the Legion Condor. The German ground element was codenamed Gruppe Imker (beekeeper) and included a variety of training and support units including Panzergruppe Drohne (drone) headed by the commander of II./Panzer Regiment.4, Oberstleutnant Wilhelm von Thoma. The initial shipment to Spain included 41 PzKpfw I Ausf A. The Panzergruppe arrived in Seville in October 1936 and was followed by additional personnel and 21 of the improved PzKpfw I Ausf B tanks. Panzergruppe Drohne set up its base in Cubas de la Sagra in the Madrid area; its role was training, not combat. The school was a battalion in size, with three tank companies and associated support units; it also contained an antitank element that eventually raised ten antitank gun companies armed with the Rheinmetall 37mm PaK 36. The Spanish Regimiento de Infantería Argel número 37 led by Comandante de Infantería D. José Pujales Carrasco was converted by their German trainers into the 1st Batallón de Carros de Combate, organized into three companies each with 16 tanks. These companies were eventually dubbed "Negrillos" (Blacks) to distinguish them from the "Rusas" (Russians) using captured Soviet T-26 tanks. The name stemmed either from the dark gray paint of the German tanks or the black berets of the German crews.

1. CV 3/35, RAGGRUPPAMENTO CARRISTI, 1938

Although some of the older CV 3/33 tankettes appear to have arrived in a scheme of brick red with small dark green splotches (*rosso ruggine, verde scurro*) the majority of the tankettes appeared in standard army gray green (*grigio verde*). This camouflage scheme sometimes was amplified with blotches of dark brown, as seen on this tankette. The regimental markings switched from the RRS to the Raggruppamento Carristi (RC) with a set of simple white geometric symbols being adopted for the four companies, with the individual tank number painted inside the symbol. In this case it identifies this vehicle as the 6th tank of 1st Company. The inset drawing shows typical examples for the 1st, 2nd, 4th, and 3rd companies (clockwise from top left).

2. CV 3/35-BREDA, RAGGRUPPAMENTO CARRISTI, 1938

This is the sole example of the CV 3/35 tankette that was upgraded with the Breda 20mm M35 cannon. The rhomboid side markings are those used by the independent company of the RC, which contained the regiment's flame-thrower tanks and other specialized types.

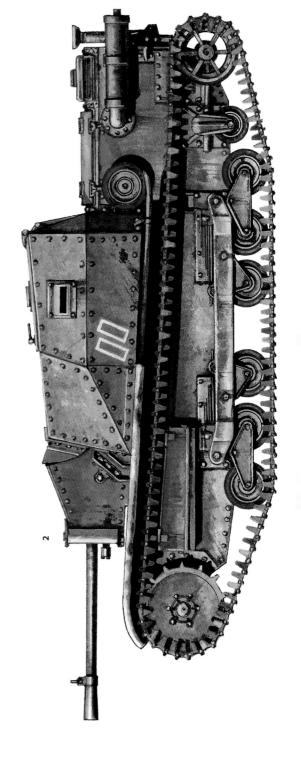

A column of PzKpfw I Ausf A tanks of the Nationalist 1st Batallón de Carros de Combate moves forward with the crew riding outside. (John Prigent Collection)

Germany eventually supplied a total of 122 tanks: 96 PzKpfw I Ausf A, 21 PzKpfw I Ausf B, 4 Befehlswagen I command tanks and one turretless training tank. Only a handful of German tankers saw regular combat action. The PzKpfw I proved to be far more robust and durable automotively than the T-26 and 93 remained in service at war's end.

The Nationalist "Negrillos" tank companies were gradually deployed into combat during the fighting around Madrid starting in early November 1936, usually in company strength to support various infantry units. They had their first encounter with T-26 tanks during the fighting around the Ciudad Universitaria. Losses in the November fighting were significant, with six tanks destroyed and 16 damaged. Although the panzers were used mainly for infantry support, they continued to bump into Republican T-26 tank and BA-3 armored-car units. During the fighting around Pozuelo in December 1936 and January 1937, over a dozen PzKpfw I tanks were knocked out fighting Soviet armored vehicles. The PzKpfw I could fire the special SmKH armor-piercing machine-gun round, but this could penetrate the T-26 only at ranges of about 120–150m. Once the Republican crews realized this they avoided close-range combat with the German tanks, and stood off where their 45mm guns were still effective; the 45mm gun on the T-26 could penetrate the PzKpfw I at ranges up to 1km. The Germans responded by deploying five 37mm PaK 36 towed antitank guns in each Spanish tank

Panzergruppe Drohne converted a single PzKpfw I Ausf A into a flame-thrower tank by mounting a small man-portable flame-thrower in place of one of the machine guns. (NARA)

company. On December 6, 1936 Von Thoma sent back an urgent report to Berlin urging that gun-armed tanks be deployed to Spain as quickly as possible, armed at least with the 20mm KwK30 gun already in use on German armored cars.

As the Spanish Civil War intensified, Stalin agreed to reinforce the Spanish contingent. A second wave of about 200 Soviet tank crews and tank specialists arrived on November 26, 1936, commanded by Kombrig D. G. Pavlov. The expansion permitted the formation of the 1a Brigada Blindada (1st Armored Brigade). Pavlov's brigade in Spain was only about a third the size of a normal Red Army light-tank brigade, with a nominal table of organization and equipment of 96 tanks, and an actual strength through most of the winter and spring fighting of seldom more than 60 tanks. As in the case of Krivoshein's units, there were not nearly enough Soviet tankers to man this unit, and as a result Spanish crews had to be used. In total, some 351 Soviet tankers served in Spain during the course of the war but, from available unit records, the total at any one time was never more than 160 men, and usually not more than 100 tankers. Pavlov's new brigade absorbed the surviving remnants of Krivoshein's tank units, which constituted its 1st Tank Battalion.

Germany sent four of these Befehlswagen I command tanks to Spain, which were a version of the PzKpfw I Ausf B but with a fixed superstructure and additional radio equipment. They were issued on a scale of one per company plus one in the battalion headquarters. The prominent St Andrew's Cross painted on the roof was an air identity mark common on Nationalist tanks to prevent strafing by friendly aircraft. (NARA)

Pavlov's brigade was prematurely pressed into action in early January 1937 with only 47 tanks on hand. The mission was to support the counteroffensive of the 12th and 14th International Brigades towards Majadahonda on January 11, 1937, on Madrid's western front. In contrast to the previous experience with the Spanish units, the cooperation with the International Brigade infantry was somewhat more successful. The tanks were very useful in overcoming the Nationalist defensive line but once the initial defensive lines were broken by the tanks and infantry, the infantry was unable to keep up with the tanks and became separated. The tanks could have penetrated the Nationalist lines more deeply but, as Arman's initial raid had shown, breakthroughs without accompanying infantry were futile. The scourge of the Republican tank force was the new German 37mm PaK 36 antitank gun; in three days of fighting, the unit lost five tanks.

The Majadahonda offensive soon ended when the Nationalist forces switched the focus of their assault on Madrid to the southeastern front along the Jarama River. Pavlov's brigade was broken up into small company-sized detachments to reinforce the Republican lines. As the French had found in World War I, the presence of tanks provided a strong psychological reinforcement to demoralized infantry, and there was great demand for tank support across the Madrid front. Even after the losses suffered in recent weeks, the brigade's strength had increased to 60 tanks as more crews became available and more tanks repaired. The Republican forces went over to the offensive, supported by Pavlov's scattered units. The Nationalist forces around Madrid had numerical tank superiority in this campaign, with about 70 tanks, but the T-26 was clearly superior to the German and Italian types.

Technical data

Type T-26 tank Model 1937 with radio (Radiyniy tank T-26 vypusk 1937 goda)

Crew 3: driver, gunner, loader

Loaded weight 9.75 metric tons

Unloaded weight 8.9 metric tons

Length 4.62m

Width 2.44m

Height 2.24m

Ground clearance 0.38m

Road speed 30 km/h

Avg. cross-country speed 10 km/h

Main gun 20-K 45mm tank gun with semi-automatic breech

Main gun ammunition 107 rounds (111 rounds in tank without radio)

Secondary armament DT 7.62mm coaxial machine gun+ DT on P-40M AA mount on turret

Ammunition 3,024 rounds (48 drums): 2,772 in tank without radio

Engine GAZ 4-cylinder, 93 hp

Range 220–240 km on roads, 130–140 km cross-country

Radio 71-TK-1 with clothesline antenna on early tanks; 71-TK-3 with whip antenna on later tanks

Armor 15mm sides, 6–10mm top

Key

1. Engine air intake
2. GAZ 4-cylinder engine
3. Radiator
4. Radiator air intake with armored grills
5. Rear turret DT 7.62mm machine gun
6. Left turret side 45mm ammunition stowage
7. 20-K 45mm tank gun with semi-automatic breech
8. Gunner's episcope
9. Gunner's telescopic sight
10. Loader's hatch with P-40M anti-aircraft machine gun mount
11. DT 7.62mm machine gun on P-40M mount
12. Turret ventilator cover
13. Loader's periscopic sight
14. Co-axial DT 7.62mm machine gun
15. Driver's controls
16. Transmission
17. Drive sprocket
18. Turret pistol port (loader's side)
19. Suspension bogie
20. Driver's seat
21. Loader's 45mm ammunition stowage
22. DT machine gun ammunition stowage bin on floor
23. Loader's seat
24. Drive train between engine and transmission
25. Idler wheel
26. Fuel tank
27. Muffler

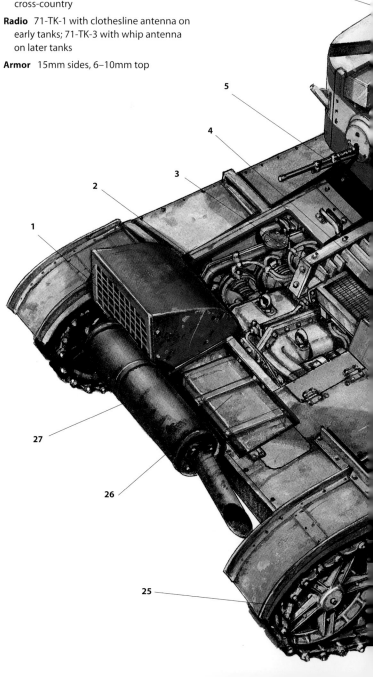

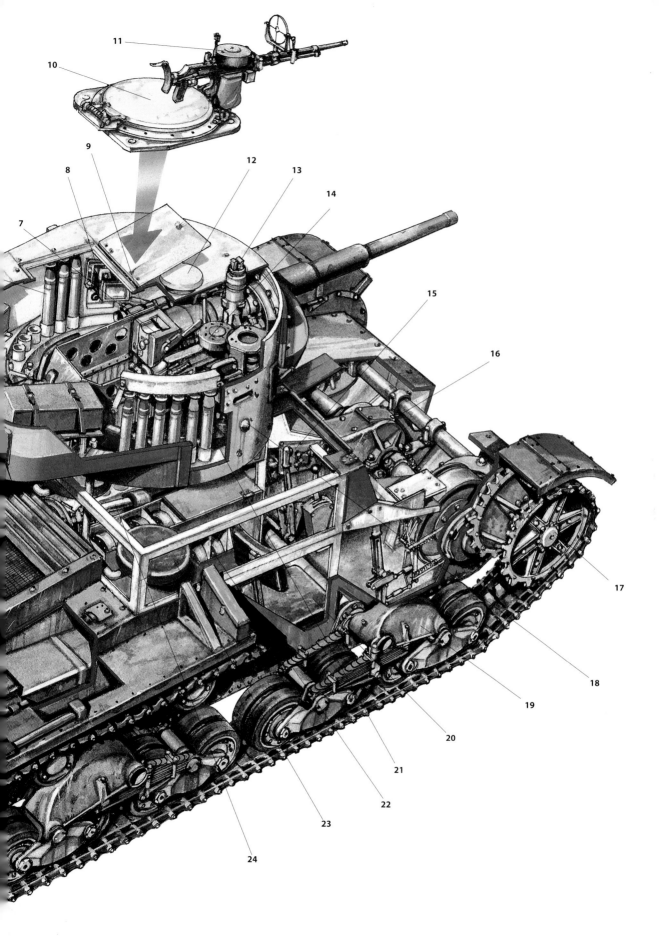

A Befehlswagen I command tank sometime after February 1938. when Franco attached the battalion to the Tercio; the Legion's Escudo marking can be seen on the superstructure above the driver's open visor. The provision of dedicated radio vehicles was due to the Wehrmacht's prescient view that radio communications were essential in coordinating modern mobile operations. (John Prigent Collection)

The Soviet advisers' report to Moscow on the Jarama operation was not favorable. The fighting cost the brigade 34 tanks, nearly 70 percent of the force committed, mainly to Nationalist antitank guns. Soviet artillery specialist Komkor (General) G. I. Kulik sarcastically remarked that the antitank gun could sweep the battlefield of tanks the same way that machine guns swept it of infantry.

In March the front shifted yet again, this time to the north of Madrid, as an Italian offensive began at Guadalajara. Two of the CTV divisions had the support of two tankette companies each. Once again, Pavlov's tanks rallied to save the day. On March 13, 1937, one of the few tank-vs-tank skirmishes took place when the Republican T-26 light tanks shot up a company of Italian CV 3/35 tankettes near Trijueque, destroying five and seriously damaging two more. There were many small tank encounters, and the Italian tankers soon learned to fear contact with the Republican rearguards defended by T-26 tanks. When the Italian CTV offensive was finally exhausted the Republicans went over to the offensive, with Pavlov's tanks in the lead. On March 18, three Republican infantry brigades with tank support routed the lead Italian units and seized the town of Brihuega. By the end of the day Pavlov's force had suffered so many casualties, to both enemy fire and mechanical problems, that of its original 60 tanks at the beginning of the Guadalajara fighting it was able to muster only nine tanks to chase the retreating Italians. The Republicans were unable to exploit their victory, achieved in no small measure due to the tank support. Tank losses were lower than in earlier campaigns: 28 tanks or about 40 percent of the force in three weeks of fighting.

Pavlov's force received a major infusion of new equipment and manpower in March 1937 with the arrival by sea of 100 new T-26 tanks. This was nearly as many tanks as had been supplied since the beginning of the Soviet intervention. The main problem was to train enough Spanish crewmen to equip them. The unfavorable view held by many Soviet officers of the Spanish tank crew led to plans to recruit tankers from the more highly-regarded International Brigades. Since there were limits on the amount of training that could be undertaken in Spain, these foreign volunteers were sent to the Soviet tank school in Gorky. Due to the influx of new tanks in the spring of 1937, it was possible to increase the number of tank battalions in Spain from three to four. These new units, and the demands from other fronts for armor support, led to the decision to organize three additional armored brigades in the spring and summer of 1937. Unlike the 1st Armored Brigade, these later brigades had only a single tank battalion, plus two battalions of locally manufactured armored cars. Manned by Spanish personnel, they did not have the mobility or firepower of the 1st Armored Brigade and were not ready until late in 1937.

Soviet Tank Shipments to Spain			
Date of Arrival	Ship	Quantity	Type
Oct 12, 1936	Komsomol	50	T-26 light tank
Nov 25, 1936	Cabo Palos	37	T-26 light tank
Nov 30, 1936	Marc Caribo	19	T-26 light tank
Mar 6, 1937	Cabo Santo Tomas	60	T-26 light tank
Mar 8, 1937	Darro	40	T-26 light tank
May 7, 1937	Cabo Palos	50	T-26 light tank
Aug 10, 1937	Cabo San Agustin	50	BT-5 fast tank
Mar 13, 1938	Gravelines	25	T-26 light tank

By the time of the Brunete offensive, the 1st Armored Brigade had filled out its three tank battalions, and Republican tank strength was 129 T-26 tanks plus 43 BA-3 and FAI armored cars. Under the plan for the offensive, the 1st and 4th battalions with 70 tanks and 20 armored cars would support the main assault by the 5th and 18th corps (one tank battalion per corps), while the 2nd Battalion with 30 tanks and 10 armored cars would support the separate offensive by the 2-bis Corps southeast of Madrid. The Brunete offensive was intended to relieve Madrid, enveloping the Nationalist forces

An interesting photo of a PzKpfw I of the 3a Compañia of the Nationalist 1st Batallón de Carros de Combate with its distinctive emblem, a skull and crossbones, probably inspired by widespread use of this symbol by the German Panzergruppe Drohne. (John Prigent Collection)

on the approaches to the city. The attack by the 18th Corps on Villanueva de la Cañada on July 6 began badly. The tank battalion advanced across an open field with the infantry from the 34th Division following behind, but the tanks were stopped about 500–600m from the town by two well-concealed antitank guns and two field guns. Four more attacks failed to overcome resistance in the town; one of the German 37mm guns had been mounted in a church steeple and was credited with a dozen tanks. The town was finally taken by the 15th Division, but the corps failed to reach its objectives during the first day of fighting. Although the 5th Corps made better progress, it too failed its main objectives. Over the next few days, the tanks were used to support the Republican infantry in a series of small local attacks, which largely failed to dislodge the reinforced Nationalist positions. Even after committing its reserve tank battalion, by July 11, 1937, the 1st Armored Brigade in the Brunete sector was reduced in strength to only 38 tanks. On July 18, the Nationalists shifted to the offensive against the exhausted and demoralized Republican forces. They proved no more able to dislodge the Republicans, and the campaign ended in stalemate.

Brunete attracted far more attention by Western military analysts than most other tank engagements in Spain during the war due to extensive press coverage. The inability of the tanks to advance in the face of enemy antitank guns was cited by many as evidence of the failure of the tank to restore mobility to warfare. Even noted British theorist B. H. Liddell Hart began to have his doubts in view of the Spanish experience. Yet, to other observers, the tanks had been poorly employed, and there was skepticism whether many lessons could be learned from the Spanish experience. British armor advocate Major-General J. F. C. Fuller remarked: "Battles are not won by clichés or Liddell-Hartisms," and he dismissed most of the press remarks about armor, attributing the tanks' poor performance to the abysmal tactics employed in Spain. Russian assessments of the lessons of the Brunete campaign paid little attention to the tank operations and focused instead on the poor quality of the Republican infantry, its continued inability to cooperate effectively with either tanks or artillery, and the inflexibility of the artillery in assisting in offensive operations. It was also pointed out that the main attack sectors had an unusually high density of antitank guns and artillery, 26.6 guns per kilometer compared to an average of 13.8 guns per kilometer on the front as a whole.

Republican T-26 Tank Casualties in Spain October 1936–August 1937

Campaign	Date	Tanks participating	Destroyed tanks	Disabled tanks	Total casualties
Madrid	Oct 26–28, 1936 Nov 28, 1936	87	16 (18.3%)	36 (41.4%)	52 (59.7%)
Jarama	Feb 5–27, 1937	47	14 (29.8%)	20 (42.6%)	34 (72.4%)
Guadalajara	Mar 9–22, 1937	72	7 (9.7%)	21 (29.2%)	28 (38.9%)
Casa del Campo	May 5–12, 1937	84	10 (11.9%)	13 (15.5%)	23 (27.3%)
Brunete	Jul 6–28, 1937	132	21 (15.9%)	26 (19.7%)	47 (35.5%)
Total		422	68 (16.1%)	116 (27.4%)	184 (43.6%)

NATIONALIST EXPANSION

Following the Brunete campaign, Franco shifted the focus of the Nationalist attack from the stiffly defended Madrid region to the isolated Asturias and Basque regions in the north. Following the Guadalajara debacle, the Italian CTV was shifted to the Asturias front along with the RRS and its four tankette companies. Curiously enough, this was a sector where Republican tanks other than the Soviet types were predominant, including Renault FT tanks. This industrial region was the center of Republican tank-building efforts. Fábrica de Trubia designed another improvised tank based on the Landesa artillery tractor. About ten were converted by Constructora Naval de Sestao and so the tank was known as the Trubia-Naval. The Renaults serving with the Army of the North included some tanks originally acquired from France, along with more recent acquisitions from Poland. Although there was no ideological affinity between the Polish and Spanish governments, Warsaw decided to sell off a great deal of old weaponry to Spain to help fund its own military modernization effort. Two shipments totaling 32 Renault FT tanks were delivered to Alicante on the Mediterranean

The Carro Trubia-Naval was the only tank produced in any significant number in Spain during the war. It was sometimes called the "Basque Tank" because of its manufacture in Bilbao. The ten tanks served with the 1o Sección de la Compañía de Carros Orugas, part of one of the battalions serving in the Republican Army of the North. (Patton Museum)

The PzKpfw I was poorly suited to tank fighting due to its machine-gun armament. Four tanks were up-armed with a Breda 20mm cannon in an enlarged turret as seen on the tank in the background here. The PzKpfw I Ausf B in the foreground is a company command tank, identifiable by the M painted on the diamond insignia on the hull front. (NARA)

on November 24, 1936, and at Santander in the north on March 3, 1937. The two Republican corps of the Army of the North each had a tank battalion. The defeat of the Army of the North in August/September 1937 led to a sudden windfall of captured tanks for the Nationalists, including 13 Renault FT and 5 Trubia tanks; Italian losses were seven tankettes and an armored car.

The firepower superiority of the Republican T-26 during the spring and summer fighting in 1937 was painfully apparent to the Nationalist tank forces and, with no hope of satisfactory tanks from Italy and Germany, local initiatives were undertaken. The Italian Breda 20mm Modelo 1935 antiaircraft gun was adapted as a tank weapon since it could penetrate 40mm of armor at a range of 250m, more than adequate against the 15mm armor of the T-26. Conversions of the PzKpfw I Ausf A took place at the Fábrica de Armas in Seville in the summer of 1937, and a total of four were completed. The turret was extended upwards to accommodate the larger gun. The Germans were extremely unhappy about the conversion, calling them "death

A rare glimpse of one of the four PzKpfw I Ausf A up-armed by the addition of a Breda M35 20mm cannon. These were allotted on a scale of one per company to provide the units with some organic antitank capability in the event a T-26 was encountered. (John Prigent Collection)

tanks" due to an opening in the turret front for the gun sight, which made the gunner vulnerable to small-arms fire. In the event, further conversions were halted as by this time enough Republican T-26 tanks had been captured to supplement the PzKpfw I. However, the Italian CTV still saw a need for a similar upgrade to give their tankette units more firepower. A single CV 3/35 was converted with the same gun and in August 1937, Nationalist headquarters authorized the conversion of 40 tankettes with the Breda cannon. However none were completed beyond the prototype.

By October 1937, the Nationalist forces had captured ten intact T-26s and many more damaged examples that could be cannibalized for parts. These were turned over to Von Thoma's training center for incorporation into the Nationalist units. Eventually there were enough intact T-26s captured that each PzKpfw I company had a single T-26 for fire support and separate

By late 1937, the Nationalist tank battalion had accumulated enough intact T-26 tanks to deploy one in each PzKpfw I platoon, and a platoon in each company. These tanks are from the 6th Company, 2nd Batallón de Carros de Combate de la Legion. (NARA)

The widespread use of captured tanks by the Nationalists led to efforts to clearly mark the T-26 with prominent insignia. This was usually a tricolor band of red/yellow/red on the turret front and rear, as seen on this Legion T-26 Model 1937 tank in 1938.

The troops of Panzergruppe Drohne stand at attention at their base at Cubas de la Sagra in front of some captured T-26 that they refurbished for the 1st Batallón de Carros de Combate de la Legion. As can be seen, some have the early form of air identification mark on their turret roof, a white St Andrew's Cross on a black background, while the tank in the foreground has the more common black cross on a white background, which was found to be more visible from the air. (NARA)

T-26 companies were gradually added. By 1938 the 1st Batallón de Carros de Combate was organized into two tactical groups, each with two companies of PzKpfw I and one company of T-26 tanks, for a total of six companies. Most of the captured Renault and Trubia tanks were rebuilt in Seville but were of such dubious utility that they were relegated mostly to training. In order to raise the prestige of the tank battalion, in February 1938 Franco assigned it to the Legion as the Bandera de Carros de Combate de la Legion, under the command of the 2o Tercio de la Legion. Under this configuration, the two tactical groups were renamed as battalions but the unit had the same strength of six companies.

The Italian RRS was reorganized in October 1937 as the Raggruppamento Carristi (RC), consisting of two weak battalions, each with two tankette companies, and a motorized infantry battalion with two sections of Italian 47mm and German 37mm antitank guns. The intention was to reorient the tankette force from an infantry support arm to a mobile force. The Raggruppamento Carristi took an active part in the brutal battle for Teruel in the winter of 1937–38 but would not see much opportunity to display mobile combat tactics until the final months of the war.

FINAL REPUBLICAN REINFORCEMENTS

The International Tank Regiment was the last Soviet tank unit deployed to Spain. By the summer of 1937 the Soviet Union had shipped 256 T-26 tanks to Spain for the various tank battalions. The last major shipment of 50 tanks

T-26 MODEL 1933, BANDERA DE CARROS DE COMBATE DE LA LEGION, CUBAS DE LA SAGRA, 1938

The captured T-26 tanks, more popularly called "Vickers" in Nationalist service, were rebuilt and repainted by Panzergruppe Drohne at their Cubas base before being incorporated into the Spanish Legion tank regiment. In ordered to prevent their misidentification as Republican tanks, they were prominently marked with the red/yellow/red flag colors of Franco's forces and usually had the turret roof painted in white with a St Andrew's Cross for air identification to prevent being attacked by Nationalist aircraft. They were often painted in camouflage colors, usually a sand or brown color over the usual Soviet dark. Inset are the unit insignia.

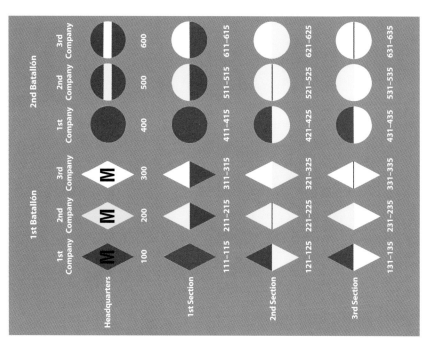

	1st Batallón			2nd Batallón		
	1st Company	2nd Company	3rd Company	1st Company	2nd Company	3rd Company
Headquarters	**M**	**M**	**M**			
	100	200	300	400	500	600
1st Section						
	111–115	211–215	311–315	411–415	511–515	611–615
2nd Section						
	121–125	221–225	321–325	421–425	521–525	621–625
3rd Section						
	131–135	231–235	331–335	431–435	531–535	631–635

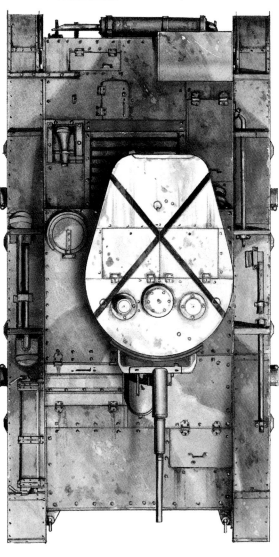

The BT-5 fast tank saw its combat debut with the International Tank Brigade at Fuentes de Ebro on October 13, 1937. This unit was manned by a mixture of Soviet crews from the 5th Kalinovsky Mechanized Corps from Naro-Fominsk, and International Brigade troops trained at Gorky in the Soviet Union. Poor planning led to a debacle and heavy losses. (NARA)

were BT-5 (Bystrykhodniy Tank: fast tank). In contrast to the T-26 light tanks, the BT-5 fast tanks were intended for deep maneuver operations, not for close infantry support. They were a license-built copy of the American Christie tank, but with a Soviet-designed turret and gun identical to that on the T-26. They were considered by the Soviet advisers to be the most modern and best tanks in Spain, and were held in reserve through the late summer and early autumn, waiting for a major opportunity to exploit their capabilities. As in the case of other Red Army units deployed to Spain, Soviet crews made up only a small fraction of the personnel in the regiment. The International Tank Regiment was allotted the cream of the Spanish trainees and the personnel from the International Brigades who had returned from the Gorky Tank School in the Soviet Union. For many of the Soviet advisers in Spain, the International Tank Regiment was the last, best hope to display the power of tanks on the modern battlefield. These hopes would be crushed in the autumn of 1937 during the Zaragoza campaign.

In early October, a Republican offensive was planned against the town of Fuentes de Ebro on the road to Zaragoza. The preparations for employing the tanks were slapdash and incompetent. The International Tank Regiment was subjected to a hasty 50km road march the night before the attack and on arriving, was informed that the tanks would carry infantry during the attack. This decision was opposed by the Soviet advisers as well as by the tank officers, who felt that it would put the infantry at too great a risk. The mission was planned in such haste that the regimental staff had no time to conduct a reconnaissance of the battlefield, and the Spanish command did not provide adequate details of the battle area or likely Nationalist antitank defenses, considering such issues "trivial." This would prove fatal to the operation.

The assault began shortly after noon. The 48 tanks of the International Tank Regiment started the attack with a salvo of their guns, and then set off at high speed "like an express train," with Spanish infantry clinging to their sides. In the din and dust of the action, many of the infantry fell off the tanks, some run over and crushed by other tanks. Crossing the friendly trenches was a fiasco; Republican infantry had not been warned, and in the confusion there was firing between the infantry and the tanks. Once beyond the friendly lines, the tanks continued to race forward, only to be forced to halt again

A BT-5 of the International Regiment after its capture at Fuentes de Ebro. This is an interesting illustration of the wheel-cum-track running gear used on the BT, which allowed the tracks to be removed and stored on the fender and the tank operated on its road wheels. The final road wheel on either side could be powered by a drive from the rear drive sprocket. This feature was only practical on hard, dry ground or roads. (John Prigent Collection)

when they reached the edge of an escarpment about three to four meters over the plains below. After a delay in finding passageways to exit to the low ground below, the tankers were alarmed to see that the terrain in front of the enemy positions was covered with sugarcane fields, crisscrossed with irrigation ditches. The tanks continued their rush forward, but became bogged down. Nationalist field guns and antitank guns began to take their toll. The advance could not press onward due to the terrain, and there was not enough infantry to hold any territory that had been gained. After exhausting their ammunition, the tanks slowly began to make their way back to the start point with little direction or control, leaving behind several tanks stuck in the mud. In total, the International Tank Regiment lost 19 of its 48 tanks in the attack, with several more damaged; a third of its tank crews were killed or wounded. An American tanker in the regiment wrote shortly after the attack: "Courage and heroism are plentiful in Spain and the Spanish people have no lack of it. What they need is tactics. And as for tactics, on 13 October, Regiment BT was bankrupt." The great expectations for the BT tank regiment had been dashed by the continuing incompetence of the Republican senior commanders in employing tanks.

The BT-5 followed the Christie design and could be run on its tracks, or the tracks removed and run on its wheels on hard road surfaces. This shows a Republican BT-5 of the International Tank Brigade during the fighting along the Ebro River in the spring of 1938. (NARA)

A pair of BT-5 fast tanks knocked out during the fighting along the Ebro near Caspe in April 1938. These were survivors of the ill-fated tank charge by the International Tank Brigade at Fuentes de Ebro on October 13, 1937. (NARA)

The fiasco at Fuentes de Ebro on October 13, 1937, was the swansong of the Soviet tank force in Spain. While Soviet tankers would continue to act as advisers, the number of Soviet tank crews continued to diminish and the force became mostly Spanish by the end of 1937. The Soviet Union ended large sales of tanks after the delivery of the International Tank Regiment's 50 BT-5 tanks. In October 1937, the head of the Republican tank forces, Colonel Sanchez Perales, initiated a reorganization and consolidation of the force. The four armored brigades, one tank regiment, and assorted small units were to be merged into two armored divisions. These should not be confused with World War II armored divisions as they were not combined arms forces, lacking organic infantry or artillery.

With the end of Soviet tank sales in early 1938, the Republican army attempted to make up for the equipment shortfalls by local production. Aside from the numerous and crude protected trucks, the Republican government had begun to build true armored cars using armor plate and designed in cooperation with Soviet specialists. The Comisaría de Armamentos y Municiones in 1937 tried to standardize the production of an efficient armored car by the Unión Naval de Levante in Valencia, called the UNL-35. This was patterned on the Soviet FAI armored car and was generally built on imported Soviet ZiS-5 or Ford Model 85 truck chassis. The first ten were ordered in February 1937 and about 200 were eventually completed. The Subsecretaría de Armamentos promoted a slightly larger armored car based on

1. BT-5, BANDERA DE CARROS DE COMBATE DE LA LEGION, CUBAS DE LA SAGRA, 1938

Following the fiasco at Fuentes de Ebro in October 1937, the Nationalists recovered several of the International Tank Brigade's BT-5 fast tanks and incorporated them into the Spanish Foreign Legion tank regiment. As was the case with most of their tanks, they received the usual red/yellow/red turret bands, and white roof with the cross of St Andrew.

2. BT-5, INTERNATIONAL TANK BRIGADE, FUENTES DE EBRO, OCTOBER 1937

This shows the typical markings of the International Tank Brigade at the time of the disastrous Fuentes de Ebro battle. The vehicle tactical marking is painted on the turret. A hull number has also been added in roman numerals, probably indicating the company.

3. BT-5, 1ST TANK DIVISION, EBRO CAMPAIGN, 1938

Prior to the Teruel fighting in late 1937, the Republican tank force was consolidated into a tank division with the surviving BT tanks in a separate regiment. In a departure from the usual practice, the turret was painted in the Republic flag colors of purple, yellow, and red. It is unclear if this was done with a BT-5 that had been recaptured from the Nationalists, or was simply a way of distinguishing the relatively rare BT tanks.

1

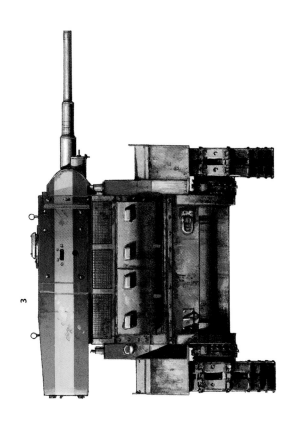

2

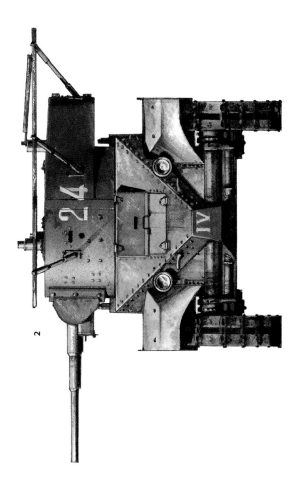

3

The final delivery batch of T-26 tanks were the Model 1937, which had the P-40-UM antiaircraft machine-gun mount on the roof. This Republican tank was captured by the Cuerpo de Ejército Marroquí and put on display with other captured equipment at an exhibition in San Sebastián in 1938. (NARA)

a three-axle truck chassis patterned on the Soviet BA-3 armored car. This was called the Blindado Modelo B.C. and was based on the Ford SD 1.5 ton truck with Thornton Truxmore Timken Third Axle Drive (6x4). About 275 were ordered and about 70–140 were completed at the Hispano-Suiza plant in Barcelona starting in 1937. Some of the later vehicles were built on imported Chevrolet 1.5 ton Series S Model 1937 and Series T 1938 trucks. The standard version was fitted with a locally designed turret with a short 37mm French SA.18 gun as used on the Renault FT tank, but a small number were fitted with the larger 45mm gun turrets from damaged Soviet tanks and armored cars. The Nationalists sponsored at least two tank-production schemes, the Ansaldo Carros de Combate de Infantería in 1937 with Italian help, and the Carros Verdeja, designed by a Spanish tank officer; however only single prototypes were built.

In May 1938, the Republican armored force had 176 tanks and 285 armored cars, and in December 1938, 126 tanks and 291 armored cars. The character of the armored force continued to shift in the direction of a road-bound force tied to armored cars and protected trucks as the inventory of tanks shrank due to combat and mechanical attrition.

The last major campaign in which Soviet tank crews participated was the bitter fighting for Teruel from December 15, 1937, to February 22, 1938. The first of the new tank divisions was committed to the fighting, consisting of two T-26 battalions, the remnants of the International Tank Regiment, and other supporting units with a total of 104 tanks. The division was not used as a unified force nor had it ever been intended to be used as such. Instead, component battalions were assigned to support various divisional attacks. The fighting took place under difficult circumstances – extremely cold weather,

The most widely manufactured armored vehicle in Spain during the war was the UNL-35 armored car built in Valencia on a light truck chassis. It was armed with a single machine gun in the hull and one in the small turret, and a pair is seen here in 1938 after being captured by the Nationalists. (NARA)

A column of derelict Republican vehicles in Madrid after the Nationalist victory in 1939. The UNL-35 armored car seen here is missing both its turret- and hull-mounted machine-guns. (Author's collection)

heavy snow, poor roads, and in mountainous country. The tank units were praised for their efforts by the infantry they supported. While the Teruel campaign has seldom attracted much attention for its tank actions, it was carefully studied by the Red Army. What was striking about the campaign was that the tank force was able to function at all. By the end of 1937 the tanks had exceeded their expected mechanical lifespan, yet the tank units were able to maintain a respectable fraction of their tanks in combat on a daily basis, and overall losses were modest under the circumstances – 24 tanks, of which seven were captured by the Nationalists. A total of 63 tanks, more than half the force, required overhaul, which was managed by the units in the field. It was a remarkable accomplishment, and reflected the growing skill of the Spanish tank crews, the maintenance units, and the tank support infrastructure created by Spanish industry. This legacy helps account for the ability of the Republican tank force to maintain its size and fighting potential for most of the remainder of 1938, in spite of the cutoff in Soviet technical aid. By the time of the summer battle along the Ebro River in 1938, the Republican tank force had been worn down to a fraction of its former size, and 17 tanks were destroyed and 18 captured in the last major Republican offensive.

The Blindado B.C. was a larger 6x4 armored car built on Ford or Chevrolet truck chassis. The usual armament was a French SA.18 37mm gun and DT machine gun in the turret, with an additional DT machine gun in the hull aside the driver. This particular example is in Nationalist hands with an Italian Lancia 1ZM armored car behind it. (NARA)

The fighting in the latter half of 1938 went badly for the Republican forces; Catalonia was cut off from the rest of the Republican-held territory and Franco's forces gradually overwhelmed the remaining strongholds. By this stage of the war, the armored forces on both sides were mechanically exhausted though they continued to be used on a small scale. In view of the indifferent performance of Italian tank units during most of the war, the Raggruppamento Carristi performed remarkably well in the campaigns in late 1938 and early 1939. It was committed as the spearhead of CTV motorized columns on deep-penetration missions, including a 200km deep raid during the final campaign in Catalonia in April 1939. Of the 157 Italian tankettes deployed in Spain, 87 were knocked out and about 70 remained at the end of the war.

LESSONS OF THE SPANISH CIVIL WAR

Most of the "lessons learned" from the Spanish Civil War were not lessons at all, but simply deductions based on flimsy or non-existent evidence bent to fit existing preconceptions. Most military analysts in the 1930s, including the military intelligence services of the Great Powers, had few firm facts about scale or conduct of tank operations in Spain. A British attaché in Spain during the war wisely warned that "the greatest caution must be used in deducing general lessons from this war: a little adroitness and it will be possible to use it to 'prove' any preconceived theory." Although the armies participating in Spain (including the Soviet, German, and Italian armies) collected extensive data from their own experiences, this material was not widely shared and much of it still has not seen the light of day more than a half-century after the event. A study at the US Army Infantry School by Captain Thomas Stark in 1939 entitled "Employment of Tanks in the Spanish Civil War" concluded that the lack of detailed information precluded any comprehensive analysis. This information gap allowed military analysts of the period to give free rein to their own prejudices on the subject of army mechanization. For nearly every lesson drawn from Spain by one group of military theorists, another can be found arguing precisely the opposite viewpoint.

Spain did not serve as "the proving ground for blitzkrieg," as it has often been described, as there were too few tanks to ever attempt large-scale tank

PZKPFW I AUSF A, BANDERA DE CARROS DE COMBATE DE LA LEGION, CUBAS DE LA SAGRA, 1938

The first batch of PzKpfw I Ausf A tanks that were delivered to Spain with Panzergruppe Drohne were painted in the Buntfarbenstrich (mottled paint pattern) consisting of No.17 earth yellow, No.28 green, and No.18 brown. When tanks were rebuilt, they were sometimes overpainted in lighter finishes more suitable for Spanish conditions, with bands of sand- or earth-colored paints. The PzKpfw I tanks eventually received similar markings to the Legion T-26, except that the turret bands were far less conspicuous, limited to a tapering quadrangle on the rear of the turret. The St Andrew's Cross marking was usually painted on the turret hatch as seen here. The Legion Escudo marking was carried adjacent to the Nationalist tricolor. The markings of the 1st Batallón were based around the diamond, while the 2nd Batallón used the circle. Colors corresponded to numbers (1 = red, 2 = yellow, and 3 = white). The top of the circle or diamond indicated company, so a circle or diamond with a red top was 1st Company, yellow was 2nd Company, etc. The lower half indicated the section, so a circle or diamond with a red bottom was 1st Section, yellow was 2nd, etc. The headquarters company was a variation on this. In the 1st Batallón, the diamond was in the company color, with a black M (Mando), while in the case of the 2nd Batallón, a red circle was used but with a horizontal band in company colors. Vehicle tactical numbers were three digit, the first indicating company, the second indicating section and third indicating the separate vehicle. In the case of the 2nd Batallón, the company numbers were 4 to 6.

The BA-6 medium-armored car was armed with the same turret and 45mm gun as the T-26 tank. This one was knocked out during the fighting along the Ebro in 1938. Spain bought 3 BA-3, 37 BA-6, and 20 FAI armored cars from the Soviet Union. (NARA)

operations. The Republican forces had the largest tank arsenal due to Soviet supplies but, contrary to the widely held belief that 1,000 or more tanks were supplied, in fact only about 300 tanks were sent to Spain. These arrived over the course of two years so on only a few occasions were Republican forces able to field more than 100 operational tanks. Usually operations were conducted by a handful of scattered companies of tanks numbering a few dozen. The Nationalist tank forces had even smaller tank contingents, which seldom operated above platoon or company level.

The second impediment to assessing the tactical importance of tanks was in the quality of the crews in Spain. Except for the Italian CTV tankette companies, the majority of Republican and Nationalist tank crews were Spanish or foreign volunteers. The training provided was rudimentary at best, and consisted of the essentials of tank operation, but little on tank tactics or tank doctrine. Senior Spanish commanders had little or no knowledge about how tank units were supposed to be used on the battlefield. As a result, tank operations in Spain were conducted by tank crews who knew scarcely more than basic operations, led by officers with little or no tactical training, on missions conceived by senior commanders who had no grasp of the tactical potential or shortcomings of tank units in combat.

This Blindado Cardé y Escoriaza is a fairly typical example of the types of protected trucks built by the Republican forces. This particular example was constructed at the well-known railroad carriage plant in Zaragoza in Aragón in September 1936. It is seen here during the fighting in the winter of 1937–38 around Teruel. (NARA)

During the final year of the war some Republican units followed the Nationalist style and painted identity bands on the tank turret, in this case the purple, yellow, and red, of the Republican flag. This BT-5 took part in the fighting on the Ebro in the spring of 1938. (NARA)

It should not have come as a surprise to anyone that tanks did not have a decisive impact on the Spanish battlefield.

While most "lessons learned" were based on dubious press accounts and ill-informed speculation, there were important exceptions. Due to its inside connections in Spain, the Red Army had an extensive collection of data on the actual conduct of tank operations during the Spanish Civil War. A Soviet General Staff in 1939 concluded that the full potential of tanks had not been displayed in Spain but that the Red Army should continue to pursue its own plans to use tanks on a mass scale regardless of the Spanish experience, due to the ambiguous lessons of the civil war. The Soviet lessons were also distorted by Stalin's grotesque political purges against the Soviet officer cadres at this time. The German army completely dismissed the tactical lessons of the Spanish experience for many of the same reasons.

A training exercise by the 1st Batallón de Carros de Combate de la Legion at the Panzergruppe Drohne training camp near Cubas de la Sagra in 1938 after a smoke grenade was thrown underneath the lead T-26 tank. (NARA)

Some 123 T-26 tanks were still intact at the end of the war. As a result, the T-26 remained in Spanish army service in dwindling numbers into the early 1960s. Here they are seen on parade being carried by White 920 tank transporters. (NARA)

Though there was little to learn about tank tactics from the Spanish experience, there were some significant technological lessons. Spain signaled the deathknell of the cheap, machine-gun-armed tank. Tank-vs-tank-fighting in World War I had been rare, so in the 1930s many armies thought that a machine gun would be adequate. The Spanish conflict showed that tank-vs-tank had become routine, so a tank gun in the 37mm range with a coaxial machine gun for antipersonnel use were the minimum acceptable tank weapons. The Spanish conflict exposed the vulnerability of the flimsy armor of most interwar tank designs. During World War I there had been few dedicated antitank weapons, but by the 1930s, the arrival of abundant and powerful infantry antitank guns in the 37–45mm range overwhelmed the armor protection of typical tanks. The parsimonious budgets of the interwar years favored lightly armored tanks, since tanks with better armor would also require more powerful engines and more robust suspensions, resulting in a rapid escalation of both purchase price and operating costs.

These trends were not entirely unexpected. By the mid-1930s France was already in the midst of adopting a new generation of infantry and cavalry tanks that would be protected against the 37mm-gun threat, and these emerged as the Renault R-35 infantry tank, Hotchkiss H-39 cavalry tank, Somua S-35 cavalry tank and the Char B1 bis battle tank by 1940. Until the civil war in Spain, both Germany and the Soviet Union relied on lightly armored tanks that were vulnerable to 37mm guns. The German army quickly appreciated the threat posed by the new guns, and had further incentive to move to thicker armor due to the poor performance of its own machine-gun armed PzKpfw I tanks against the gun-armed Soviet T-26 tank. The German army began to shift to better-protected medium tanks such as the PzKpfw III. The Soviet Union's response was more extreme, and proved to be a watershed in tank design: the legendary T-34 tank. The original Red Army 1937 requirement for its new A-20 cavalry tank was unexceptional and had the same 45mm gun, with only marginally better armor protection than the BT cavalry tank used in Spain. In 1938, Soviet tank designers debriefed a number of Spanish Civil War veterans and concluded that the next-generation cavalry tank would have to be proof against the current 37mm gun. Furthermore, the Soviet designers concluded that other armies would follow the same path and up-armor their tanks in similar fashion. So to deal with the threat posed by future enemy tanks, the new Soviet cavalry tank would have to be armed with a weapon more powerful than the 37mm gun or its Soviet 45mm equivalent to defeat the future enemy tank armor. The Soviet designers applied one of the critical paradigms of technological innovation to the design – that to prevail on the battlefield, the new tank had to be based on an appreciation of the future threat. The A-20 was redesigned and emerged in 1940–41 as the T-34 tank.

The T-34 extended the three primary attributes of tank design – armor, firepower, and mobility – in a well-balanced package not previously seen anywhere else. So, for example, while contemporary French infantry tanks like the R-35 and British infantry tanks like the Matilda I had excellent armored protection, they were deficient in both firepower and mobility. British cruiser tanks had excellent mobility, but poor armor and mediocre firepower. French battle tanks like the Char B1 bis had good armor protection and firepower, but mediocre mobility. German medium tanks such as the PzKpfw III had a good balance of armor, firepower, and mobility, but not enough to deal with the T-34. When it first appeared in combat in June 1941, the T-34 proved to be a major shock to the Wehrmacht, which was expecting to encounter an adversary equipped with tanks of the Spanish Civil War generation. The poor performance of German tanks and antitank guns against the T-34 set off an arms race on the Russian Front that had

One of the odder footnotes of the Spanish Civil War armor battles was the use of a few Blindado B.C. by the Wehrmacht in the opening phases of Operation *Barbarossa* in Russia in June 1941. About 20 of these vehicles had crossed the border from Spain into France in 1939 and were subsequently used by the French army in 1940. They were captured by the Germans in 1940 and put back into service. (Author's collection)

repercussions in every other theater of the European war. The German response, the Panther medium tank and the PaK 40 75mm antitank gun, would prove to be the bane of Allied tank forces elsewhere, such as the Allied campaigns in France in 1944. The T-34 set the standard for tank design in World War II based on the technological lessons of the Spanish Civil War.

FURTHER READING

There has been a flurry of writing on tanks in the Spanish Civil War in Spain in recent years, centered on the new Spanish defense magazine *Revista Española de Historia Militar* and its publisher, Quirón Ediciones in Valladolid. The bibliography below lists only a fraction of the articles dealing with this subject published over the past few years.

The primary archival source for this book was the splendid collection of documents obtained from the Russian State Military Archives (RGVA) by Mary Habeck at Yale University and currently housed at the Manuscript and Archives branch of Sterling Memorial Library. The Russian State Military Archive Collection (RSMAC-Group 1670) deals with Soviet–German military collaboration in the 1920s and with Soviet military participation in the Spanish Civil War. There are hundreds of thousands of pages of Russian reports on the Spanish Civil War, including detailed accounts of arms delivery, tactical experiences, after-action reports, and a wealth of other material. For a more extensive description of this unique resource, my JSMS article listed below has extensive endnotes on the reports. The Red Army also published an extensive series of articles on the lessons of the Spanish Civil War in the late 1930s in their journals *Voenniy Mysl and Voenno-istorichesskiy zhurnal*, and I used the collections of the Lehman Library, School of International Affairs, Columbia University. I also looked through the attaché reports of the US Army in the Military Intelligence Division records at the US National Archives and Records Administration (NARA).

Articles
Alvarez, José, "Tank Warfare during the Rif Rebellion," *Armor*, January–February 1997, pp. 26–27
Caiti, Pierangelo & Pirella, Alberto, "The Role of Italian Armor in the Spanish Civil War," *Armor*, May–June 1986, pp. 40–44
Candil, Antonio, "Soviet Armor in Spain: Aid Mission to Republicans Testing Doctrine and Equipment," *Armor*, March–April 1999, pp. 31–38
Crespo Fresno, Carlos & Franco, Lucas Molina, "El desconocido «carro veloce CV-3/35» Breda," *Revista Española de Historia Militar*, January 2000, pp. 54–55
Daley, John, "The Theory and Practice of Armored Warfare in Spain, October 1936–February 1937," *Armor*, March–April 1999, pp. 30, 39–40
Daley, John, "Soviet and German Advisors Put Doctrine to the Test: Tanks in the Siege of Madrid," *Armor*, May–June 1999, pp. 33–38
Franco, Lucas Molina & Garcia, José Manrique, "Carros de combata autóctonos en el Ejército Espagñol 1936–39," *Revista Española de Historia Militar*, January–February 2003, pp. 51–60
Franco, Lucas Molina; Garcia, José Manrique & Pérez, Artemio Mortera, "Tanques Soviéticos para el Ejército Nacional 1936–1939," *Revista Española de Historia Militar*, March 2003, pp. 136–149
Franco, Lucas Molina, "Blindados en la Revolucion de Asturias 1934," *Revista Española de Historia Militar*, October 2004, pp. 207–2010

Harvey, A. D., "The Spanish Civil War as Seen by British Officers," *RUSI Journal*, August 1996, pp. 65–67

Kolomiets, Maksim & Moshchanskiy, Ilya, "Tanki Ispanskoi Respubliki," *Tankomaster*, Nos. 2–3 1998, pp. 2–9

Lalinde, Leonardo Blanco, "La Empresa Carde y Escoriaza: Producion de material military durante la Guerra Civil Española," *Revista Española de Historia Militar*, July–August 2002, pp. 44–50

Manrique, J. M., "Algo mas sobre los «carros italianos» en 1936/39," *Revista Española de Historia Militar*, May 2000, pp. 169–174, September 2000, pp. 299–303

Surlémont, Raymond, "Armour on Rails in the Spanish Civil War," *Military Modelling*, July 1995, pp. 31–34

Surlémont, Raymond, "Blindés Italiens en terre d'Espagne 1936–1939," *Tank Museum News*, No. 45, pp. 4–11

Zaloga, Steven, "Soviet Tank Operations in the Spanish Civil War," *Journal of Slavic Military Studies*, September 1999, pp. 134–162

Books

Albert, F. C., *Carros de Combate y Vehiculos Blindados de la Guerra 1936–1939*, Borras (1980)

Duaso, Josep Maria Mata & Gutiérrez, Francisco Marín, *Blindados autóctonos en la Guerra Civil Española*, Galland (2008)

Estes, Kenneth, *History in Dispute: The Spanish Civil War*, St. James (2004)

Franco, Lucas Molina & Garcia, José Manrique, *Blindados Allemanes en el Ejército de Franco*, Galland (2008)

Franco, Lucas Molina & Garcia, José Manrique, *Blindados Italianos en el Ejército de Franco*, Galland (2007)

Franco, Lucas Molina & Garcia, José Manrique, *Blindados Soviéticos en el Ejército de Franco*, Galland (2007)

Franco, Lucas Molina & Garcia, José Manrique, *Soldiers of Von Thoma: Legion Condor Ground Forces in the Spanish Civil War 1936–1939*, Schiffer (2008)

Habeck, Mary, *Storm of Steel: The Development of Armor Doctrine in Germany and the Soviet Union 1919–1939*, Cornell (2003)

Howson, Gerald, *Arms for Spain: The Untold Story of the Spanish Civil War*, John Murray (1998)

Jentz, Thomas, *Panzerkampfwagen I No. 1–2*, Panzertracks (2002)

Lyubarskiy, S., *Nekotorye operativno-takticheskie vyvody iz opyta voyni v Ispanii*, Red Army General Staff (1939)

Marin, Francisco & Mata, Josep Maria, *Blindados: Los Medios Blindados de Ruedas en Espana: Un Siglo de Historia Vol. 1*, Quiron (2002)

Marin, Francisco & Mata, Josep Maria, *Carros de Combate y Vehículos de cadenzas del Ejército Espagñol*, Revista Española de Historia Militar, Part-work (2004–2005)

de Mazarrasa, Javier, *Los Carros de Combate en la Guerra de España 1936–1939*, Quiron (1998)

Royo, Oscar Bruña, *Vehiculos Acorazados en el Tercia Vol. 1*, Quiron (1998)

Strasheim, Rainer & Prigent, John, et al., *Panzerwaffe: The Evolution of the Panzerwaffe to the Fall of Poland 1939*, Ian Allen (2007)

Svirin, Mikhail & Kolomiyets, Maksim, *T-26 Legkiy Tank*, Frontovaya Illyustratsiya (2003)

Taibo, Javier, *Blindados y Carros de Combate Españoles 1906–1939*, Defensa (1996)

INDEX

Note: letters in bold refer to plates and illustrations.